UNDERSEA UNIVERSITY™

The Ultimate Beach Book

by **Robin Epstein** · with **Sharon Katz Cooper** Consultant

SCHOLASTIC INC.

New York Toronto London Auckland Sydney Mexico City New Delhi Hong Kong Buenos Aires

Robin Epstein
WRITER

Robin lives in New York and has written on topics ranging from police investigations to juggling.

Sharon Katz Cooper
CONSULTANT

Sharon is the education specialist for the National Museum of Natural History's Ocean Hall, set to open in 2008. She lives in Virginia with her husband, Jason, and son, Reuven.

ISBN: 0-439-71194-0

Copyright © 2005 by Scholastic Inc.

Illustrators: Yancey C. Labat, Ed Shems

Photos:

Front cover: MedioImages (RF)/Getty Images. Back cover: Rubberball Productions (RF)/Getty Images. Title page: Image source (RF)/Getty Images.

Page 2: Photodisc Green (RF)/Getty Images. Pages 4, 5, and 6: Amla Sanghvi. Page 7: (background) Andrea Menotti; (quartz) Mark A. Schneider/Photo Researchers; (mica) Andrew J. Martinez/Photo Researchers; (amethyst and feldspar) Mark A. Schneider/Photo Researchers. Pages 8 and 9: Elizabeth H. Kennair and L. Bruce Railsback, Department of Geology, University of Georgia. Page 11: World Sand Sculpting Academy WSSA 2005. Page 12: www.TeamSandtastic.com. Page 13: (castle, bust, and cathedral) Copyright World Sand Sculpting Academy WSSA 2005; (coral-reef scene) www.TeamSandtastic.com. Page 15: (surfer) Royalty-Free/Corbis. Page 16: Darren Hester/pixelperfectdigital.com. Page 17: Andrea Menotti. Page 19: Andrew J. Martinez/Photo Researchers. Page 20: (jetties) Andrea Menotti; (beach parts) image*after. Page 23: Andrea Menotti. Page 24: (Singing Beach) Gabriel Ricard; (Dead Sea) Richard T. Nowitz/Corbis. Page 25: (Perissa) G. Rossenbach/zefa/Corbis; (black sand) Loes Modderman; (Green Sand Beach) Douglas Peebles/Corbis; (green sand) Elizabeth H. Kennair and L. Bruce Railsback, Department of Geology, University of Georgia; (Red Sand Beach) Neil Rabinowitz/Corbis; (red sand) Douglas Peebles/Corbis; (Banzai Pipeline) Tony Arruza/Corbis. Page 26: Andrea Menotti. Page 27: (green anole) David Kearnes/SeaPics.com; (gopher tortoise) Ken Lucas/Visuals Unlimited. (Wilson's plover) Charles Melton/Visuals Unlimited; (oystercatcher) Arthur Morris/Visuals Unlimited. Page 28: (goose barnacles) Doug Perrine/SeaPics.com; (hermit crab) Royalty-Free/Corbis. Page 29: (shield limpet) Brandon Cole; (purple shore crab) Adam Jones/Visuals Unlimited; (sea slug) Royalty-Free/Corbis. Page 30: Jesse Castaldi. Page 31: (A) Doug Perrine/SeaPics.com; (B) Brandon Cole; (C and D) NOAA National Estuarine Research Reserve Collection; (E) Kate Guthrie, Edmonds Discovery Programs. Page 32: (top) National Oceanic & Atmospheric Adminstration (NOAA); (bottom) Ken Lucas/Visuals Unlimited. Page 33: (top) Jeremy Stafford-Deitsch/SeaPics.com; (bottom) Stan Elems/Visuals Unlimited. Page 34: (top) Doug Perrine/SeaPics.com; (bottom) Doug Perrine/SeaPics.com. Page 36: (nematode and gastrotrich) Matthew Hooge, The University of Maine; (tardigrade) Photo Researchers. Page 37: (rotifer and turbellarian) Matthew Hooge, The University of Maine; (kinorhynch) David Scharf/SPL/Photo Researchers. Page 38: (microscope) PBNJ Productions/Brand X Pictures (RF)/Getty Images. Page 39: (A, D, and E) Matthew Hooge, The University of Maine; (B and C) Ron Shimek; (F) David Gems, University College London. Page 40: (comb jelly) Richard Herrmann/SeaPics.com; (sea nettle) David Wrobel/SeaPics.com; (moon jelly) Masa Ushioda/SeaPics.com. Page 41: (isopod) Espen Rekdal/SeaPics.com; (sea sponge) NOAA; (A) Visuals Unlimited; (B) James D. Watt/SeaPics.com; (C) Marty Snyderman/Visuals Unlimited; (D) Daniel W. Gotshall/Visuals Unlimited. Page 42: (seaweed) David Wrobel/Visuals Unlimited; (kelp holdfast) David Wrobel/SeaPics.com; (kelp zoom) Phillip Colla/SeaPics.com. Page 43: (kelp forest) Doug Perrine/SeaPics.com; (seaweed) Andrea Menotti. Page 44: (top) Arthur Morris/Corbis; (bottom) Peter Scoones/SPL/Photo Researchers. Page 45: (serrated bill) Flip De Nooyer/Foto Natura/Minden Picture; (hooked bill) David Shen/SeaPics.com; (seagull) Andrea Menotti; (pelican) Hal Beral/V&W/SeaPics.com. Page 46: (frigatebird) Hubert Stadler/Corbis; (tropicbird) Wolfgang Kaehler/Corbis; (tern) NOAA National Estuarine Research Reserve Collection. Page 47: Courtesy of Dr. Schreiber. Page 48: Digital Vision (RF)/Getty Images.

12 11 10 9 8 7 6 5 4 3 2   7 8 9/0

Printed in the U.S.A.

First Scholastic printing, October 2005

The publisher has made every effort to ensure that the activities in this book are safe when done as instructed. Adults should provide guidance and supervision whenever the activity requires.

Table of Contents

page 10

Hit the

Y ou can *hear* it. You can *smell* it. You can even *feel* it between your toes! What is this thing that will excite *all* your senses (and might even leave you soaking wet)?

It's the part of the ocean closest to land—the beach! And the number of amazing natural events that go on there in a single day is as intense as the noontime sun! In this book, you'll explore the areas where the water meets the sand, and you'll meet the fascinating creatures that make these places home.

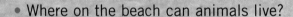

You'll also find the answers to questions like these:

• What is sand made of?

• Does the sand on a beach stay there forever?

• What causes rip currents?

• Where does driftwood come from?

• Where on the beach can animals live?

• Do all jellies have painful stings?

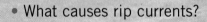

• What kinds of birds live near the beach?

Beach!

Shore, It's a Beach

It's an ideal location to enter a sand-castle contest. It's by far the best spot to take a leisurely stroll as you're wading in the ocean. And it's really the *only* place to play beach volleyball. But what *is* a beach, exactly?

Where the ocean meets the land, a *shore* is created. If the shore is covered in loose particles, like sand, then that area is called a *beach*. Not all shores are covered with sand, though, which means they're not *all* beaches. For example, if the ocean meets some really high rocks, what forms is known as a *cliff*. And if the ocean crashes into soft wetland that's covered in grass, it's called a *marsh*.

But *this* is a BEACH BOOK! So, in this book, you'll dig deep into the world of sandy shores. You'll find out how the water waves, and you'll discover the creatures that call the beach their home. So put on some sunscreen and get ready for some wet 'n' wild adventures!

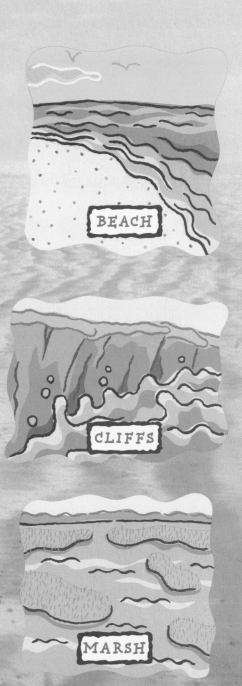

BEACH

CLIFFS

MARSH

What's in Your Undersea Kit?

This cool kit contains the very latest in sand-castle technology. With sculptable sand and nifty sand-shaping tools, you'll be able to create your own little piece of beach! Check out what you've got below, and turn to page 10 to start sculpting!

Moldable Sand

It looks like normal sand…it feels like normal sand…it even collects under your fingernails like normal sand! But the sand in your Undersea Kit is special, because it always stays sculptably wet! This will allow you to mold and shape it just like you would with wet sand at the beach.

Rake, Spade, Sand Castle Molds, and Wooden Paddle

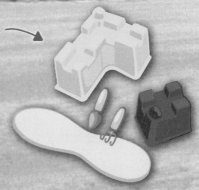

Every good builder needs a set of tools. Your kit contains two sand castle molds of different shapes and sizes. Once you pack the sand into these molds, you can even out the bottom using the wooden paddle. Then, with the rake and spade, you'll be able to dig through the sand to create moats and tunnels around your castles!

Seashells and Wooden Sailboat

What would a seascape be without some seashells and a toy boat? After you've created your sandy beach scene, adorn it with these amazing little accessories.

The Undersea University Website

Surf over to www.scholastic.com/undersea to find a sand-sational new game! Just don't forget the password on the right.

WEB-SURFING PASSWORD

BEACHBUM

PART 1: Forces That Form the Beach

If you've ever watched your biggest, best sand castle get wiped out by the waves at the beach, you've already got an idea of the kinds of forces at play there. In this part of the book, get ready to find out exactly *how* all those seaside forces work!

Zany, Grainy Sand

When you hear the word "beach," what's the first thing that comes to mind? (After "Whoo-hoo, summertime!") If you said "sand," you're not alone. It's just one of those things that sticks with you after a day at the beach! But you might be wondering...

What's Sand Made Of?

Sand is made mainly of rocks and shells—really, *really* small pieces of rocks and shells! Over millions of years, waves pound against these rocks and shells, grinding them to a fine powder the size of salt grains (about 0.05 to 2 mm across).

quartz

mica

feldspar

You can guess what kind of rock a piece of sand started out as just by looking at it. If the sand glimmers, it could be made from quartz rock. Sparkling white or black flakes could be mica (a shiny kind of rock). White, pink, and red grains of sand are probably made of feldspar (a multi-colored stone). And occasionally you'll even see purplish sand, which comes from amethyst and other minerals.

amethyst

Scattering Sand

The wind and waves keep sand on the move. Scoop a handful of sand in a fixed spot on a beach—say in front of one particular palm tree—then go back a year later and take another handful from *exactly the same spot*, and you'll be picking up entirely different grains of sand!

Look Out Below!

Sea Quest

What You Need
- Your sand smarts

It may seem hard to believe, but when you walk on a beach, it's like you're stepping back into history. That's because each grain of sand started out as something else! By carefully examining the magnified sand grains in this Sea Quest, see if you can trace the origin of the sand!

What You Do

On these two pages, you'll see photos of sand collected from all over the world, shown at the sand's actual size, along with magnified views of the sand grains. Match each type of sand to the material you think most of the grains are made of! When you've made your guesses, check your answers on page 48.

A. Tiny shells left behind by single-celled creatures

B. Hardened lava

C. Seashells

D. Pebbles

E. Pure quartz

F. Quartz and other minerals

1 Florida

2 Hawaii

3 Australia

4 California

5 Connecticut

6 Morocco

9

Beachfront Property

What You Need

- Sand Castle Kit **UNDERSEA**
- 2 small bowls
- ½ cup of salt

As any great architect will tell you, when you're constructing a building, the materials you use are extraordinarily important. And if you're going to the effort of building something in the first place, you want to make sure it's a strong structure, right? Then try this Sea Quest to find out the key to creating a spectacular palace of sand!

What You Do

I. Open the bag of sand from your Sand Castle Kit and empty it into a small bowl. Flatten and smooth it with your wooden paddle until it looks like a beach. Now, use your spade to dig a hole in the sand. How does it hold up?

3. In another bowl, pour in ½ cup of salt and smooth it so it's flat. Now, try to dig a hole in the salt like you did in the sand. Can you do it? What happens?

2. Now pack one of your sand castle molds with sand, then carefully remove the mold. How does your castle look?

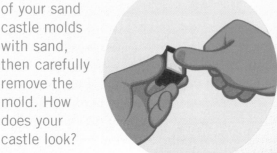

4. Pack one of your sand castle molds with salt this time, then remove the mold. What happens to your castle?

Sea the Point?

What goes between bricks to help bind them together? Wet cement! And what keeps snowflakes packed into a snowball? Water molecules! Moisture helps hold things together, and the same is true when water's mixed with sand.

As you found in this Sea Quest, the sand in your Sand Castle Kit works just like wet sand—*and* it won't dry out. When you tried building a castle out of the totally dry salt, the grains flowed apart because there was no water to hold them together.

Imagine if you were a crab trying to tunnel into a pile of salt—or dry sand. Your tunnel would close up right behind you! That's why tunneling animals need to live in wet sand, which will hold the shape of their burrows. But that's not the only reason animals live in the wet sand at a beach. Marine animals that breathe through gills need the water to survive!

Bucket Patrol

Some beaches have sand-sculpting contests where professional artists go head to head with talented beach bums to see who can build the best sand castle or sculpture. One trick employed by the pros is to keep an ample supply of water close by to keep the sand as wet as possible while they're molding it. They either keep water stocked in nearby buckets, or they dig a very deep hole in the sand not far from their creation (when you dig deeply enough into the sand at a beach, eventually you'll hit water).

To build a really tall tower of sand, one technique is to stack "pancakes" of very wet sand, one on top of the other, like bricks. As you just learned, the wetness between those pancakes cements them together and helps them hold their shape!

Sand castles under construction at a competition in Japan

Ultimate Sand Sculptures!

Sand castles aren't limited to the ones you make with buckets at the beach—the possibilities are endless. Sand sculptures can even be taller than their creators!

How Do They Do That?

To make sand sculptures that are taller than a person, regular buckets just don't cut it. First, sand sculptors compact the wet sand into shallow wooden boxes that look sort of like sandboxes at a playground. This part takes a *lot* of shoveling. They stack these boxes one on top of the other, with each one smaller and smaller, until they have a pyramid-shaped tower. Then, they remove the boxes layer by layer, leaving a block of sand to sculpt.

To carve out their sand, sand sculptors use all sorts of tools, including cake-decorating equipment and even dental instruments for the really detailed parts! Because the sand has been compacted so well, they can carve out tunnels and even create arches.

It's hard to believe, but a sand sculpture—just sand and water—can last for over a year, as long as nobody touches it!

A sand-sculpting group called Sandtastic built up this pyramid layer by layer, then removed the wood to start carving. This sculpture contains about 240 tons of sand, and it earned the team a Guinness World Record in sand sculpture!

Super Sculpture Gallery

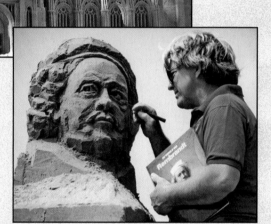

A team of five sand sculptors made this amazing sand-sculpture replica of a cathedral in the Netherlands.

How does your best sand castle compare to this one? It was made by a sand sculptor in Holland.

Gerry K. Kirk, a world-renowned sand sculptor and president of the World Sand Sculpting Academy (WSSA), sculpted this bust of the famous painter Rembrandt out of sand. The WSSA holds sand-sculpture competitions and events around the world.

Sandtastic, the creators of the sculpture on the left, sculpted this coral-reef scene out of sand to attract attention in a shopping mall.

Doing the Wave!

Have you ever been in a stadium when the crowd got so excited it started doing "the wave"? When a wave gets going, you can practically feel the energy moving through the crowd as the wave rolls across each section and people jump to their feet! Well, a wave in the ocean works in a similar way—except instead of the energy moving through *people*, it moves through water!

That's right—ocean waves are the result of energy moving through water. Though it may *look* like the water is moving, what you're really seeing when you watch waves approach the shore is the movement of *energy*.

And where does all that energy come from? Usually, the energy comes from wind blowing on the water's surface, but it can *also* come from underwater earthquakes. A wave caused by a quake is called a tsunami (soo-NAHM-ee), which is a Japanese word that means "harbor wave."

The Anatomy of a Wave

Here's the basic structure of a wave:

Crest: the highest part or peak of the wave.

Trough: the low part of the wave, or the "valley" between two waves.

Wave Height: the distance from the top to the bottom of the wave, between its crest and its trough.

Wavelength: the distance between the crest of one wave and the crest of the next wave.

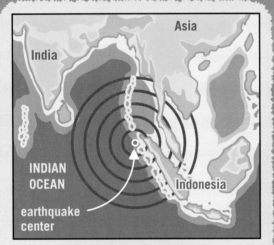

The Big Bad Wave

One of the biggest tsunamis in history happened on December 26, 2004, in the Indian Ocean. It all began with a big undersea earthquake off the western coast of Sumatra, Indonesia. The energy released by the quake created waves that began rippling outward, picking up speed and height as they neared various coastlines.

With a tsunami, the more powerful the earthquake, the stronger the waves will be. The stronger the waves, the greater the destruction. Scientists reported that this earthquake lasted nearly ten minutes (most last only a few seconds!), and it caused the whole planet to vibrate at least a few centimeters. The damage it caused made this one of the worst natural disasters in modern history.

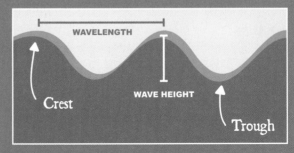

Surf's Up!

If the first thing that comes to mind when you hear the word "surfing" is the internet, it's time to shut down the computer and get out into the sunshine! Surfing, the kind that involves big waves and a board, has been a favorite activity of extreme-sports fans for decades. It's all about using the energy of a breaking wave—or a *tripping* wave, actually!

What a Trip!

Out at sea where the water's deep, a wave glides freely across the water. But as the wave nears the shore and the water gets shallower, the wave starts to trip on the seafloor!

Think of what happens when you're running full force and then have to stop really fast—though your feet may stop, your head still jerks forward. This is exactly what happens to a wave as it hits the shore. Since the top of the wave is still moving quickly, the wave's "head" trips over its "feet" and breaks onto the shore. The area where waves break is called the *surf*, and the region between the breaking waves and the shore is the *surf zone*.

Gimme a Break!

Surfing is when you use a board (a traditional surfboard or a smaller boogie board) to catch the edge of a wave as it's breaking. The energy of that break—when the wave begins tripping on the seafloor—is what propels the board and by extension YOU, the board-rider, forward!

To catch a wave, surfers paddle out just beyond the surf zone, before waves have begun to break, and lie on their surfboards, watching the horizon for incoming waves. As soon as a wave begins to trip under the surfboard, the surfer pops up into a standing position and rides the wave to shore.

The Motion of the Ocean

It's not hard to make waves. Toss a pebble into a puddle, drop a rubber ducky into a tub, or do a cannonball into a swimming pool, and you'll see the rippling effect. But as those ripples travel outward, the *water* stays put, as you learned on page 14. Hard to believe? See it for yourself with this Sea Quest!

What You Need

- Thick piece of rope about 6 feet (2 m) long (a jump rope will work)
- Doorknob

What You Do

1. Tie one end of a long piece of rope around a doorknob.

2. Pick up the other end and back away until the rope is stretched from the doorknob to your hand.

3. Flick your hand up and then down to create a wave in the rope, then watch as it travels toward the doorknob. Try it again, moving your hand up and down faster or slower, and check out the waves you can make!

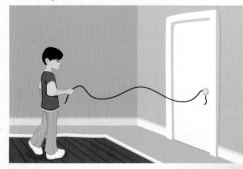

Sea the Point?

You should have seen that each wave you made traveled down the length of the rope. But the rope itself didn't travel! It only moved up and down, and *not* in the direction of the wave.

Why? Because the only thing that *was* traveling was the energy, in the form of the wave. And this is exactly how waves in the water work. It may look like the water is moving toward you in a wave, but you're really seeing *energy* moving through the water!

Waves in water, just like the waves in your rope, are caused by traveling energy.

This'll Tide You Over

Ever set down your beach towel high above the water, only to find the water just a few feet away a couple hours later? That's what happens when high tide comes in! But what makes it happen? Read on!

You're Pulling My Leg!

The Moon travels around the Earth once a day, causing two high tides: one when the Moon is closest to that part of the Earth, the other when it's on the opposite side of the planet. (To find out why this happens, check out the next Sea Quest.)

high tide

During a high tide, the water on the Earth actually bulges out away from the planet (and climbs up the beach). Low tide is just the opposite—it happens when the Moon is halfway between you and the other side of the Earth, creating a high tide somewhere else and a *low tide* where you are. Then, instead of bulging, the water slides back down the beach.

low tide

Spring Forward, Neap Back

When the Earth, Sun, and Moon are in a line, which happens twice a month, there's a *spring tide*, which is an especially high and low tide. This happens because the Sun's gravity pulls in the same direction as the Moon's, making the tides extra big.

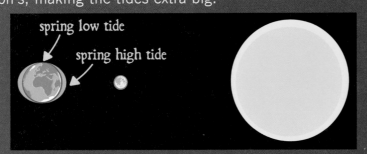
spring low tide
spring high tide

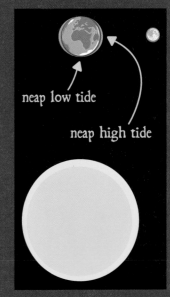
neap low tide
neap high tide

And when the Moon and Sun are arranged as shown on the right, their pulls cancel each other out a little, so the tides are much smaller than usual. These are called *neap tides*, and they happen twice a month, too.

Turn the Tides

When it's high tide at a beach near you, the Moon could be on the opposite side of the planet. How can the Moon cause a high tide if it's not right overhead? In this Sea Quest, you'll get to *be* the Moon and see for yourself!

What You Need

- 2 pieces of paper
- Scissors
- Tape
- Ruler
- Piece of string about 2 feet (61 cm) long

What You Do

1. Cut a strip from the long edge of a piece of paper and tape its ends together, forming a loop.

2. Fold the rest of the paper in half. At the folded edge, draw a semi-circle that extends out about 1¼ inches (3 cm) from the crease. Cut around your semi-circle to get a circle that's 2½ inches (6 cm) across. That circle will represent the Earth.

3. Place your Earth in the middle of a second sheet of paper. Set your paper loop around the Earth, so the Earth is centered inside it. The paper loop represents the oceans surrounding the Earth.

EARTH

4. Tape the top of your loop down to the piece of paper. Then tape a piece of string to the opposite side of your loop (the side closest to you).

5. Now that you've set up your Earth and its surrounding oceans, it's time to see what the Moon's gravity does! Pull the string gently toward you, and inch the Earth toward you a little, too. It's as if you're the Moon pulling on the Earth and its oceans! What happens to the shape of the oceans around the Earth?

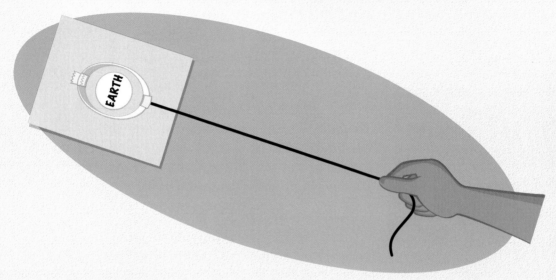

Sea the Point?

Now you know what it feels like to be the Moon! When you tugged on the string, you imitated the pull of the Moon's gravity. As you saw, the force of that pull turned the loop into an oval shape, creating a bulge on the part of the loop nearest you. That bulge is a high tide. When you moved the Earth a little closer to you, you imitated the Moon's pull on the Earth itself. This created a bulge of water on the opposite side of the Earth, too (another high tide).

If you were really the Moon, you would travel around the Earth once a day. As you moved, there would always be a high tide on the side nearest you and another on the side farthest from you. So each part of the Earth would get a high tide twice a day—once when you're close, and once when you're far!

You probably noticed that the sides of your paper loop were pulled in close to the paper circle. These are the places where the Earth experiences low tides.

Canada's Bay of Fundy, shown here, has the biggest difference between high and low tides in the world!

Beach Under Construction

Erosion, the wearing away of the beach by wind and waves, keeps the sand in constant motion. As a result, the beach is remodeled on a daily (if not hourly) basis!

Sand is collecting on the right side of this jetty and getting pulled away from the left side (probably to collect next to another jetty nearby).

Erosion's a Real Drag

Because erosion pulls the sand off the beach, some seaside towns try to stop this by building *jetties*, which are piles of rocks, sand bags, or concrete that extend out toward the sea. Jetties collect sand that would otherwise get pulled out to sea, preventing the beach from washing away.

There's only one problem: All the sand that collects against the jetty is coming from another part of the beach! So before long, another jetty has to be built to keep sand from drifting too far. This leads to a domino effect: Put up one jetty, then add another next to it, then add another next to it...

The Perfect Figure for the Beach

Even though beaches are always changing, their general shape stays the same. There's the dry, soft part of the beach you have to trudge through to get to the water, which is called the *backshore*, because it's the farthest from the water. Then there's the place you set your towels if you want them to stay dry when the tide rises. This part of the backshore, just above where the highest waves hit, is called the *berm*.

Finally, there's the part of the beach closest to the water, with wet, hard sand, where you can wade and stroll. This area, called the *foreshore*, is very narrow when the tide is in, and broad when the tide is out.

A *Rip* in the Waves

When a wave crashes on the shore, it brings lots of water with it. So how does all that water get back to sea? Sometimes, it travels back to the ocean along fast-moving currents called *rip currents*.

What Causes Rip Currents?

As soon as waves crash on the shore, the water starts heading back out to sea. Often there's a high area of sand on the seafloor near the shore that will slow the water down as it travels away from the beach. This is called a *sandbar*. But if there's a dip in that bar, the water all rushes through it—it's like a high-speed expressway back out to the ocean! This stream of rushing water is the rip current.

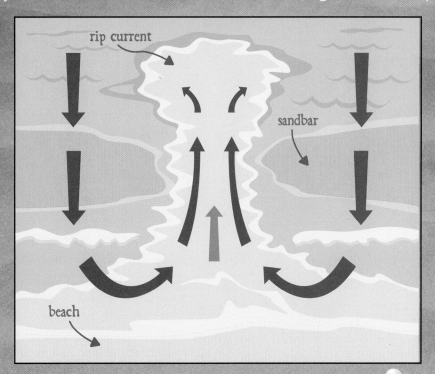

rip current

sandbar

beach

Now You See It...

Rip currents are often especially strong after storms, and there are usually warnings or red flags posted at the beach when there are dangerous rip currents. But what happens if you find yourself in one anyway? Just swim parallel to the shore, since this way you'll move out of the path of the current.

Let 'Er Rip!

Sea Quest

Forget about making a tempest in a teapot—in this Sea Quest, you'll create a rip current in a baking pan! Now that you know how a rip current works (see page 21), you can make your own version.

(see page 21)

What You Need
- Baking pan (about 9 by 13 inches)
- Sculptable sand UNDERSEA
- Water
- Ruler

What You Do

1. Scrunch your sand against the shorter end of a baking pan in the shape of a slope. This will be your beach.

2. Pour water into your pan until it reaches halfway up the beach.

3. Now hold a ruler at the end of your pan across from the beach. Nudge the ruler forward in small movements to send waves toward your beach.

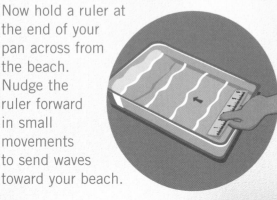

4. After you've made a few waves, check out how the water travels. After it splashes up onto your beach, where does it go? How does it get back out "to sea"?

Sea the Point?

Congratulations, ocean explorer—you just produced two rip currents! As you saw, once the water crashed on your beach, it needed to find an escape route, and it made its exit along the sides of the baking pan. That's just like what happens with real rip currents, which often form along jetties (piles of rocks that extend from the beach out to sea).

Also, you probably noticed that particles of sand from your shore washed out to sea in the rip current along with the water. That's how rip currents are frequently spotted at the beach, too—people see particularly muddy-looking currents of water and recognize the rip!

Beachcomber's Delight!

If you take a walk along the beach, you might find lots of treasures lying in the sand—but probably *not* the kind that would fill a pirate's chest! Chances are, you'll find shells, driftwood, seaweed, jellies, and lots of other *natural* treasures that were carried onto the beach by waves. Check out the cool stuff that "washed up" on this page!

Driftwood may come from branches blown off nearby trees during storms or from trees along a distant shore.

This peach pit was probably part of someone's picnic. Anything that gets dropped into the ocean can wash up on the beach.

Sea glass starts out as litter, when a bottle is tossed into the water by a careless person. Eventually, that bottle will smash into pieces, and the pieces will get smoothed out by sand and waves until they look like frosty gems.

Seaweed of all shapes and colors turns up on the beach. The seaweed shown here has air-filled bubbles at its ends that can be fun to pop!

Beachcombing Challenge

mini Quest

Which items in the checklist below can you find on the right? Check your answers on page 48.

❶ ❷ ❸ ❹

Beachcomber's Checklist:

☐ **A) Sea bean** (also known as a drift seed). These come from trees and vines that grow along tropical shores and in rainforests all over the world.

☐ **B) Mermaid's purse**. This is actually an egg case that used to hold a baby skate (a type of fish related to sharks).

☐ **C) Jellyfish**. When jellies wash up on the beach, they often lose their tentacles.

☐ **D) Part of a fish's spine**. Bones from fish can be found washed ashore.

☐ **E) Crab**. After a crab has died, there are many creatures on the beach that eat its meat, but some parts of it get left behind.

☐ **F) Sponge**. Sponges' rubbery skeletons often wash ashore, looking like brown clumps of seaweed.

Amazing Beaches Around the World

All beaches are *not* created equal. Check out the gorgeous, stunning, and downright weird features of these beautiful beaches from around the world!

Singing Beach

SINGING BEACH— Manchester-by-the-Sea, Massachusetts

The sand can't be too wet or too dry, but when conditions are just right, the sand "sings" (or squeaks) when you walk on it. How's that for cool? No one's exactly sure what causes it, but it seems to happen when the sand grains are all about the same size.

DEAD SEA SHORES—Middle East

The water of the Dead Sea is so salty, nothing but algae can live there. About 1,370 feet (417 m) below sea level, the Dead Sea is the lowest exposed area on Earth—this means that all of the water nearby flows into it. Add lots of heat to evaporate the water, and the Dead Sea is left full of mineral salts. People use these salts and the black mud on the Dead Sea's shores for spa treatments!

Dead Sea shores

PERISSA BEACH—Santorini, Greece

When a volcano erupted on the island of Santorini in the 15th century B.C., the center of the island collapsed into the sea, forming a big water-filled basin. The sand of Santorini's black beaches is made from a type of volcanic rock called obsidian, which was created by magma that flowed to the sea and then cooled rapidly. Eventually the rock was reduced to bits of fine black sand by the waves.

Perissa Beach

huge Banzai Pipeline wave

NORTH SHORE—
Oahu, Hawaii

Oahu's North Shore is a surfer's paradise! The Banzai Pipeline is legendary for its waves, which can be both awe-inspiring and dangerous. During the winter, the oceans churn and the waves curl up to 30 feet (9 m) high before they hammer into the sandy shores.

Green Sand Beach

GREEN SAND BEACH—
Big Island, Hawaii

Green Sand Beach is one of the most interesting beaches in the world, not just because it's the southernmost beach in the United States. The sand contains olivine, a green volcanic rock. Individual nuggets of olivine can be picked up by the handful on this beach!

Kaihalulu

RED SAND BEACH—
Maui, Hawaii

On the island of Maui you'll find Kaihalulu (kai-hah-LOO-loo), also called Red Sand Beach. The sand has a dark red color because it comes from a crumbling cinder cone (a hill made out of ashes around a volcanic vent) that runs around the bay.

PART 2: Beach Creatures

Can you imagine getting to be at the beach *every single day*? The creatures you'll learn about in Part 2 of this book do exactly that. They've figured out a variety of ways to live on, around, and even *under* the beach!

The Dunes of Hazard!

Picture yourself standing on a beach as a cool breeze comes off the ocean. Nice, right? Okay, now imagine that the wind picks up and starts blowing harder. Good. Now add *more* wind. Imagine it gusting all around you, whipping so hard it blows the floppy beach hats right off the old ladies' heads!

If that wind is strong enough to send Grandma's hat skyward, imagine what it's doing to the tiny particles of sand at your feet! When sand is picked up and thrown around by the wind, it often drops in piles behind the beach that are known as *dunes*, which grow larger over time.

Beach Homes

First, grasses take root in the sand dunes and help stabilize the sand piles, so the sand doesn't move around as much. Then, animals move in!

Who are the residents of this seaside property? Well, there are birds, snakes, lizards, and tortoises—just to name a few! But you'll only be able to find them if you know what you're looking for. Check out a few dune-dwelling creatures on the next page.

Green anole (uh-NO-lee): This little lizard, found in the Southeastern part of the United States, loves to hang out and lie in the Sun. But even life at the beach can be stressful, and when the anole starts "feeling the heat," it can turn from bright green to brown!

green anole

gopher tortoise

Gopher tortoise: With its shovel-like front legs, the gopher tortoise is often called a "wildlife landlord" because the HUGE burrows it makes in the sand are home to animals like mice, foxes, skunks, possums, rabbits, quail, burrowing owls, and frogs! Biologists have found some burrows as big as 40 feet (12 m) long and 10 feet (3 m) wide! But despite all the hard digging these tortoises do, they maintain a dainty diet, favoring low-growing grasses and herbs.

Wilson's plover: This small shorebird has a short, thick, dark bill, medium-gray upper parts, and white underpants...whoops! White underparts, that is! They mostly eat crabs, crayfish, and shrimp, and when they're looking for mates, the male Wilson's plover will droop his wings and spread his tail feathers in a little display for the female he's trying to impress!

Wilson's plover

American oystercatcher

American oystercatcher: Talk about a cool-looking bird! This large black-and-white bird has a bright orange beak. And if its looks don't impress you, its call certainly will, since it shrieks, "KLEEEEEP, KLEEEEP, KLEEEEP!" These birds love to eat shelled creatures like clams, snails, and, of course, oysters! They'll hammer at the shells until they break them apart to grab the meat inside.

Living on the Edge!

Tide pools are big puddles of water that collect in the rocky hollows by the edge of the ocean. The seawater splashes in and out of these pools as the tide rises and falls, which means their water level, temperature, and saltiness change throughout the day.

Even though they don't sound like very comfortable places to live, tide pools are usually full of life! Turns out that the rocky surroundings provide a lot of little hiding places for various creatures to perch in. And since there are so many creatures around, other animals are drawn to the spot because they smell dinner!

Meet the Neighbors

Goose Barnacles: These odd-looking creatures get their name from their resemblance to geese—check out those long necks! People actually used to think these barnacles would be geese when they grew up! But barnacles are spineless creatures that remain barnacles all their lives.

Inside their shells, barnacles have soft bodies with heads and legs. When they find a good place to hang out, like a rock in a tide pool, they cement their heads to the rock and wait for food to float by. Their feathery legs stick out of the tops of their shells, and when food comes near, goose barnacles use their legs to kick it right into their mouths!

goose barnacles

Hermit Crabs: Imagine if you had to carry your home on your back, and find a new one every time you outgrew it! That's the life of a hermit crab. These creatures have soft bodies, so they have to hunt for abandoned shells to live inside.

hermit crab

Finding the perfect shell isn't easy, and hermit crabs are always on the lookout for "upgrades." If they have to, they'll even eat a snail just to take its shell! Once a hermit crab has spotted the perfect shell, it hasn't won the battle yet—if another crab has spotted the shell, too, they may fight for days before the winner gets to move in!

Shield Limpets: These spineless, shelled creatures hang out on tide-pool rocks. If they're touched, they clamp down like suction cups—it isn't easy to pry a limpet from a rock! Under their shells, limpets have a tongue-like *radula* that scrapes off the algae they like to eat. The color of their shells, which varies from brown to green to white, depends on the kind of algae they eat!

shield limpet

purple shore crab

Purple Shore Crabs: If something cleaned up your room in the middle of the night, it'd be a pretty welcome visitor, wouldn't it? Well, that's just what the purple shore crab does at the beach! At night, it helps keep beaches clean by chowing down on dead animals. That's an impressive feat for a crab that only grows up to about 2 inches (5 cm) long!

Sea Slugs: These shell-less snails are called *nudibranches*, which means "naked gill." They're so frilly and colorful that you might think they just sit around and look pretty all day— but actually, these slugs are fierce predators! They munch on sponges, corals, barnacles, and even other sea slugs.

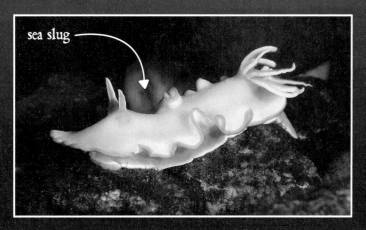

sea slug

Here's another cool thing—every sea slug is both male *and* female! That makes finding a mate a lot easier, since every other sea slug is a possible partner.

Standing the Test of Tide Pools

Sea Quest

You just met all sorts of creatures that live in tide pools, but don't let that fool you—a tide pool is not an easy place to live! All these creatures have to survive the changes in water level, temperature, and saltiness, not to mention the crashing waves. How do they do it? It's all about being adaptable!

What You Do

Each of the creatures you met on pages 28–29 is perfectly suited to survive the brutal conditions of tide-pool life. For each creature, list the adaptations that help it survive! When you've got them all, check your answers on page 48.

Adaptations:

A. Will eat another animal out of its home to get a home for itself

B. Hangs on tight to avoid being tossed around by crashing waves

C. Moves into crevices or overhangs to stay safe

D. Is covered in mucus that keeps it from drying out

E. Can close up its "home" for protection against predators and splashing water

tide pool

1 Goose Barnacle: ___ ___

2 Shield Limpet: ___ ___

3 Sea Slug: ___ ___

4 Hermit Crab: ___ ___

5 Purple Shore Crab: ___

Life's Grand on the Sand!

When you toss down your towel at the beach, you're joining a community of year-round residents. All sorts of creatures live on and under the sand—meet four of them on these two pages!

Did I Just See a Crab?

If you're on a beach on the east coast of the United States and suddenly feel something running across your foot—but you hadn't seen anything beforehand—it just might have been a **ghost crab**! This crab is just a couple inches long, and its name comes from its ability to blend in with the sand.

ghost crab

These speedy crabs can run up to ten miles per hour (16 km/h), and they have periscope eyes that stick up from their heads and swivel around, letting them see all 360 degrees around them. Their speed and all-seeing eyes help protect these crabs from predators like seagulls and dogs.

And even though you might not be able to see a ghost crab, you just might be able to hear one if the beach is quiet—they make three different sounds! They rap the sand with their claws, they rub their legs together like a cricket, and they make a strange bubbling sound, which scientists think comes from their gills.

ghost shrimp

A Shrimp out of Water

It's unlikely you'll see a **ghost shrimp**, because these animals are constantly burrowing in the sand. They dig down as far as 30 inches (76 cm) deep, and their tunnels are used by other small creatures for protection from predators—and as a place to store leftover food!

Like all shrimp, the ghost shrimp needs water to breathe—but if it has to spend a little while in dry sand, it can survive without water for up to six days! How long can *you* hold your breath?

Fiddler on the Sand

Though they don't play music, **fiddler crab** males have one small claw for gathering food and one large claw that some people think looks like a fiddle! It's used to wrestle other males and attract females. Guy crabs wave their claws to challenge other males to fight—and this actually works to impress the girl fiddlers! Female fiddlers just have two small claws.

fiddler crab

During low tides, fiddler crabs use their claws to sift through the mud to collect bits of food from the dead and decaying plants and animals in it. Though it might seem nasty to us, this stuff is full of nutrients the crabs need to survive.

During high tides, the fiddlers stay in their complex systems of tunnels, which can have several entrances! Their burrows provide not only a cool, shady place to hang out during high tide, but also protection from predators like fish, raccoons, and marine birds. Fiddlers often roll up a ball of mud to plug their burrows before the tide comes in, keeping a tiny pocket of air trapped inside for them to breathe—these crabs need both air and water to survive.

This Beach Has Fleas!

When is a flea not a flea? When it's a crab! The **sand flea** is also called a *mole crab*, because first, it *is* a crab, and second, it digs like a mole in the sand! If you dig down into the sand, you might find one of these little creatures, but it'll dive right back down immediately. That's because sand fleas like to stay underground, where they're safe from predators and from waves that could pull them into the water.

sand flea

Sand fleas don't have claws like other crabs, so they use their tails to burrow in the sand. Pay close attention and you'll see that these crabs always move backward, not sideways like most crabs!

I See Sea Turtles

As you'd expect from anything with the word "sea" in its name, sea turtles spend most of their time in the water. But, even though they're clumsy on land, they have to come onto the beach to nest. Turtles can swim more than a thousand miles to get from their feeding grounds to their nesting grounds each year!

When it's time to nest, the female sea turtles come ashore to lay sixty to a hundred eggs, each the size of a golf ball. After about two months, the babies hatch at night, when there are fewer predators. Then, they immediately run toward the water (as fast as a turtle can run, that is!).

When the baby sea turtles get to the surf, they dive into a wave and ride out to sea. They then swim continuously for the next twenty-four to forty-eight hours in a swimming marathon, to get out to deeper water where they're safest!

baby sea turtle ⟶

Stranger Danger

Unfortunately, sea turtles have become endangered. Because of development on the beach, the destruction of their natural habitats, and getting tangled in nets set by fisheries, the number of sea turtles has dwindled.

But scientists are working on "turtle-excluder" devices to help prevent the turtles from getting caught up in the fisheries' nets. And volunteers have even pitched in to keep beaches clean, protect nests, and help make sure that hatchlings make it into the ocean!

Beating the Odds

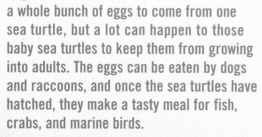

A hundred eggs might seem like a whole bunch of eggs to come from one sea turtle, but a lot can happen to those baby sea turtles to keep them from growing into adults. The eggs can be eaten by dogs and raccoons, and once the sea turtles have hatched, they make a tasty meal for fish, crabs, and marine birds.

Out of the 100 eggs this sea turtle is laying, how many do you think will grow up into adult sea turtles?

A) Fifty or more

B) About twenty five

C) About ten

D) Two or less

Check your answer on page 48!

Mamma Mia, Meiofauna!

Have you ever packed someone in the sand? Or have *you* ever gotten buried up to your ears? You probably thought you were surrounded by nothing but little sand grains—but actually, lurking within that sand were *thousands* of tiny creatures! Amazing, no? It's hard to spot these creatures with the naked eye, since they grow to a maximum of about a millimeter long, but if you check out the sand with a microscope, you'll find them! These tiny, sand-dwelling creatures are called *meiofauna* (MAY-oh-fah-nuh), which means "small creatures."

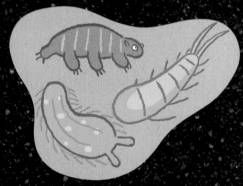

For meiofauna to thrive among the sand grains, there must be enough space between the grains of sand to hold the water the organisms need to survive. In general, the more space there is between the grains of sand, the more diversity you'll find among these tiny creatures.

Clean Up Your Act

The waves bring in all sorts of bacteria, plankton, and decaying stuff from the ocean. So why does the sand seem so clean? Turns out many of the organisms that live between the grains of sand act like little vacuum cleaners, sucking up other organisms that have died there. They actually play a key role in keeping the sand clean!

If I Were a Sand Man...

So, what does a creature need to survive between the grains of sand? First of all, it definitely helps to have a long, worm-like shape to slither between the particles. Second, grippers or claws are great for hanging onto the grains of sand, since most meiofauna can't swim. And a shell or some scales to act as armor are a big help among all those hard, bumpy grains of sand. Turn the page to meet some meiofauna firsthand!

Meet the Meiofauna

There are literally thousands of kinds of meiofauna in sand around the world! Here are just a few types:

Nematodes: These tiny, round worms live all over the world—in salt water, fresh water, and on land. In fact, they're one of the most common creatures on Earth! The nematodes that live in the sand protect themselves with a flexible cuticle (like the skin around your fingernails), which allows them to keep on wrigglin' without getting banged up by the sand grains.

nematode

tardigrade

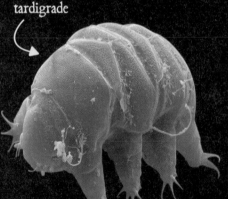

Tardigrades: These creatures, sometimes called "water bears" because they appear to have legs like a bear when seen through a microscope, are protected from the rough sand by their rigid, boxy bodies. What's really incredible about tardigrades is that they can basically freeze themselves for protection against dry conditions! They do this by replacing the water in their cell membranes with sugar. This lets them survive for years without eating or drinking, until their environment is comfortable again.

Gastrotrichs (GAS-tro-tricks): These beauties have hairy bellies to help them glide over sand, and they have scales for protection, too. They also have up to 250 sticky tubes on their tails which they can use to glue themselves onto sand grains. Just don't try to keep a gastrotrich for a pet—they only live for a total of three to twenty-one days.

gastrotrich's sticky tubes

Rotifers: Like little break dancers, rotifers move by spinning the hair-like cilia on their heads. (Their name comes from the Latin word meaning "wheel-bearer," since the whirling cilia look like a wheel.) These creatures mostly eat dead and decaying organic materials, but some rotifers even eat each other!

Some species of rotifers consist *only* of females—there are no males at all! The female rotifers lay eggs, and their daughters hatch from them, with no males involved.

rotifer

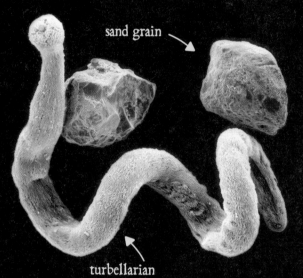

sand grain

turbellarian

Turbellarians: These wormy meiofauna have sausage-like bodies that they can squeeze into the smallest crevices. They can even retract their heads into their bodies if it's a *really* tight squeeze! They move by vibrating the tiny cilia that cover their bodies, and the slime they produce allows them to slide along any surface.

These creatures can live for a long time without food, but they'll start shrinking as their bodies begin digesting their own tissue to survive!

Kinorhynchs (KIN-or-inks): These microscopic, spiny-headed worms are sometimes called "mud dragons," maybe because they wear body armor—spines help protect them from getting crushed and keep them afloat in water.

To get their food, kinorhynchs use a long tongue-like *proboscis* covered in little hooks. The hooks latch on to the bacteria and other tiny particles these creatures eat. Once the kinorhynch has gathered enough food, it turns the proboscis inside out, collapsing it inside its head, to get at the food!

kinorhynch's proboscis

Think you know your meiofauna? Turn the page to put your new knowledge to the test!

Meiofauna Matching

Now that you've met some meiofauna, let's see how well you can pick them out of a microscope!

What You Do

On the previous two pages, you saw what some meiofauna look like as seen with a *scanning electron microscope* (SEM), a special kind of high-tech microscope that gives a 3-D view of tiny things. But meiofauna can also be seen through regular microscopes with glass lenses, like the ones you might use in science class.

If you saw the meiofauna on the right under your microscope, could you identify each one based on what you learned on pages 36–37? When you think you've got them all, check your answers on page 48!

1. Tardigrade
2. Rotifer
3. Nematode
4. Kinorhynch
5. Turbellarian
6. Gastrotrich

Life at Sea!

There are all sorts of creatures amid the waves of the seashore (not to mention human beings!). You probably already know about jellies, for one. But do all jellies sting? And what else is in the water with you?

One Hairy Comb!

Comb jellies float near the water's surface, but technically they aren't "true" jellies. That's because instead of having tentacles, they're covered in tiny hairs called *cilia* that help them move around in the water. Lucky for you, "brushing" past this comb is no problem, since they can't sting!

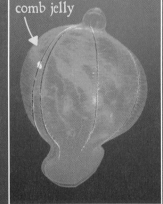
comb jelly

sea nettle

Float Like a Butterfly, Sting Like a...

It may look pretty and frilly, but don't be fooled by the **sea nettle**! A sea nettle's tentacles are coated with stinger cells. And as soon as those tentacles touch the jelly's prey—KAPOW—the stinging cells paralyze the creature, and the tentacles move the prey into the sea nettle's mouth. Lucky for you, the sea nettle eats small, drifting creatures, not people!

Moon-Made Jelly

Unlike their jelly brothers, who capture food with stinging tentacles, **moon jellies** capture the tiny animals they eat with the mucus on the surface of their bodies. And when a moon jelly has had a hefty meal, you can see the food packed in its stomach through its clear body! These jellies, which look like mushrooms or flying saucers, can grow up to 18 inches (46 cm) across. Moon jellies can sting, too, but their sting is so mild that most people don't even feel it.

moon jelly

I Spy an Isopod!

isopod

Jellies aren't the only creatures out there in the surf. Turn over a rock on the seafloor near the shore and you might find **isopods**, which look like big versions of the roly-poly pill bugs you can find under rocks on land. Isopods can also live among the seaweed near docks. Their camouflage pattern helps them blend in with the environment, making it hard for hungry fish to find them!

Since isopods only grow to less than an inch long, they'd be tossed about by the waves if it weren't for tiny claws on each leg that help them cling to the seaweed in the water. When they want to swim, their paddle-shaped back legs help them move around.

Who Wears the Square Pants in This Family?

A **sea sponge** might not make a very good pet, but these creatures really are, well, *creatures*! Some sponges stay low to the seafloor and cover the surfaces of rocks

sea sponge

like moss on land. Other types of sponges are free-standing and often grow into large, vertical tubes.

Sea sponges may be animals, but they don't swim, sting, or bite. They stay attached to the same spot on the seafloor all their lives, and from there, they suck in the water around them, filtering out tiny bits of plants and animals to eat.

mini Quest

Looks Can Be Deceiving

Creatures without backbones, called *invertebrates*, are sometimes such simple organisms that you can barely tell they're animals. Sea sponges are just one example of invertebrates that look more like a plant than a pet. Can you identify which of the following pictures is a plant and which is an animal? Check your answers on page 48!

A B C D

Weeds of the Sea

Yech! What was that slimy green stuff that just floated past you in the ocean? Fear not! It was probably seaweed, which is really just the name of a type of algae. Seaweed is often green, but not always—it can be red or brown, too!

seaweed

Not Even a Plant!

Despite its plant-like features, seaweed is not a plant of any sort, since it doesn't have roots that absorb water and nutrients from the soil. Instead, because all the parts of the seaweed are in contact with the water, they take up fluids, nutrients, and gases directly from the water itself!

However, like true plants, seaweeds use a process called *photosynthesis* to convert energy from sunlight into the food they need for growth. Within their cells, seaweeds have the green pigment *chlorophyll*, which absorbs the sunlight needed for photosynthesis. (Chlorophyll is also responsible for the green color of many seaweeds.)

Floats are the gas-filled structures that help the seaweed float.

Like the human backbone, the **stipe** of seaweed is its main stem, which supports the whole structure.

Most seaweed grows on the seafloor and can anchor there thanks to root-like parts called **holdfasts**.

Blades, the leafy extensions on seaweed, help absorb sunlight for photosynthesis.

That's One Giant Category of Algae

Seaweed comes in all shapes and sizes, ranging from the microscopic to the gigantic—in fact, there are huge "kelp forests" full of seaweed. Imagine getting lost in a forest like that!

Kelp forests are found in cool, shallow coastal waters all over the world. Kelp can grow to 200 feet (70 m) long, and entire ecosystems grow up around it. These are the "rainforests" of the sea!

Chowin' Down on Seaweed

Fans of sushi will tell you how seaweed can make a great meal. But they're not the *only* ones who enjoy snacking on it. Seaweed's a valuable food source for all sorts of creatures, from fish to hermit crabs. It also provides shelter and a home for numerous fish, invertebrates, birds, and mammals, too!

kelp forest

Algae comes in all shapes and colors. Here are just a few types you might find washed up on a beach!

BUBBLE QUIZ

Carrageenan is a product made from seaweed. It's a gum-like material that helps make food thick and creamy. Which of the following foods use extracts from seaweed in their ingredients?

A. Ice cream   **B.** Coffee creamer

C. Toothpaste   **D.** Whipping cream

E. Pudding   **F.** All of the above

Check your answer on page 48!

Beaks at the Beach:
Marine Birds!

Your average backyard bird would never be able to fish for food in the water, much less swim! But over the years, marine birds have adapted to make their lives by the ocean much breezier.

Webbed Wonders

If the floor of your home were always wet, you'd probably adjust your footgear accordingly. Marine birds have certainly gotten wise to this idea—check out the webbing on their feet! Most birds have separated toes, but if you take a gander at the feet of *marine* birds, you'll find webbing that connects their "toes."

Why the webbing? Well, though most birds only perch on tree branches, marine birds spend lots of time on the water looking for food. They use their feet like paddles, and the webbing allows them to propel themselves along the water very rapidly.

webbed feet of a puffin

Fatty, But Not Too Salty

You've probably heard that "cream rises to the top" because of its fat content. As it turns out, marine birds are especially fatty to help keep them afloat in the water. That extra layer of fat helps keep them warm, too.

Because they're bobbing in salty seawater, marine birds also have a gland located just above their eyes that helps them get rid of all that extra salt.

albatrosses floating on the water

Bill, Please!

Since marine birds eat a lot of slippery fish, they have special bills that help them keep a tight grip on their dinner. Some of these birds have hooked upper bill tips, which function almost like a spoon. Others have bills with serrated edges, like the edge of a knife.

hooked bill

serrated bill

Gabby Gulls

There are more than fifty types of gulls that fly around by the sea. Chances are, even if you don't see them at first, you'll *hear* them, since when these birds of a feather flock together, they're VERY NOISY! Gulls are incredibly common along the coast, and they'll eat just about anything, from fish to trash!

seagull

Pouch Potatoes

You think *your* mother carries a big purse? Imagine what a baby pelican must think about *its* mom! Pelicans have giant pouches under their bills that can hold more than twice the capacity of their stomachs. Talk about having a little extra storage space!

pelican's giant pouch

Pelicans live along coasts all over the world and build their nests in trees close to the beach. But when they spot food—look out!—because they make big plunging dives into the water to scoop up their fish. Understandably, baby pelicans can't pull off such dangerous maneuvers. But a baby's got to eat, so the mother pelican feeds her child by spitting up some of her own food. Now that's what you call love!

The *Fast* and the **Furious**

Though seagulls and pelicans are perhaps the best-known marine birds, there are many other frequent flyers that make a life by the sea. Here are a few:

Frigatebirds: These birds, which live around the Gulf of Mexico and the Caribbean, are fantastic flyers, since their wingspan is nearly 8 feet (3 m) long. It also helps that they're quite light, and that they have forked tails which help them change directions quickly. Frigate birds can even pluck a fish out of the water in mid-flight!

frigatebird

Frigatebirds can be bullies to other birds: They chase them until they drop their food, then they scoop it up to eat it themselves!

tropicbird and its baby

Tropicbirds: These graceful, tropical seabirds cruise the open ocean for fish. They especially love to eat squid, crustaceans, and flying fish. When the birds are young, they spend all their time at sea. As a result, scientists who track tropicbirds don't know much about them!

However, they come ashore to nest once they reach maturity, so scientists have studied their nesting behavior. And because tropicbirds nest on small islands that are predator-free, they've never learned to be scared of the scientists tracking them!

Terns: With long, gray wings and webbed feet, terns are very similar to gulls. However, they're slightly smaller and have sharp-pointed bills and forked tails. These differences allow terns to move more quickly than gulls, and let them hover in the air without flapping their wings.

Terns are expert fishers that hover over a spot in the ocean, plunging into the water as soon as they see a small fish to catch. But, because their feet are so small, they're not great swimmers, so they don't stay in the water one second longer than needed to catch a mouthful of food!

tern

Ornithologist
Dr. Betty Anne Schreiber

Dr. Betty Anne Schreiber works in the Bird Department in the National Museum of Natural History at the Smithsonian Institution. She travels to Christmas Island and Johnston Island, in the Pacific Ocean, twice a year to do her research. By studying frigatebirds, tropicbirds, and terns, Dr. Schreiber also learns about the health of our oceans. If the birds are doing well and raising healthy young, it means fish are plentiful and the ocean is healthy.

Question: What's a typical day like when you're out in the field?

Answer: Working in the tropics, we get up before dawn, since it's really hot during the day. We're working from first light till about 11 a.m., and from 3 p.m. till dark. We try not to work on the birds in the hot mid-day sunlight, because the baby birds need their mothers to protect them from the Sun.

Q: How do you catch a bird?

A: One thing about seabirds is that they've always lived on these islands where man hasn't been, so they don't have a fear of you. We usually use a long-handled net to catch the frigatebirds. You can get right up to them and put out the net. They might screech a little, but it's pretty easy to handle them!

Q: What do you study once you've caught them?

A: We take weights every year. Are the birds lighter than usual? Weight can be a monitor for pollution in the environment!

Q: What's the most interesting thing about the tropicbirds?

A: They're faithful to one another! You tag them, and you find that from year to year, they come back to the same nest. Also, when a chick leaves the nest, it takes off on its own and doesn't come back to its parents. Somehow that chick goes out there all by itself and learns how to feed without any sort of experience— and it survives!

Wave Goodbye!

Just like every day at the beach has to come to an end, this page marks the end of your Undersea U beach adventure! But as you pack up your beach bag, think about all the cool things you learned about life by the seaside!

You now know what sand is made of. You became an expert on waves, you learned how to surf, and you now understand the pull of the tides. You also learned about the dangers of rip currents, about the difficulties of living in a tide pool, and about all the creatures you share the beach with.

Next time you find yourself on the beach, see how many beach creatures you can spot—and see if you can use your new sand-castle expertise to build a real seaside masterpiece!

THE ANSWER KEY

▶ Pages 8–9: Look Out Below!

1) E   **2)** B   **3)** A   **4)** F   **5)** D   **6)** C

▶ Page 23: Beachcombing Challenge

1) B   **2)** C   **3)** D   **4)** E

▶ Pages 30–31: Standing the Test of Tide Pools

1) B, E   **2)** B, E   **3)** C, D   **4)** A, C   **5)** C

▶ Page 34: Beating the Odds

D. Only one or two sea turtles from this nest of eggs will probably survive and grow to adulthood.

▶ Pages 38–39: Meiofauna Matching

1) E   **2)** C   **3)** F   **4)** B   **5)** A   **6)** D

▶ Page 41: Looks Can Be Deceiving

A. Coralline algae—plant
B. Sponge—animal
C. Soft coral—animal
D. Red algae—plant

▶ Page 43: Bubble Quiz

F. All of the above! Hard to believe, but carrageenan is used in all of these delicious foods to give them their creamy texture!